# How Fast Is a Cheetah?

BY KURT WALDENDORF

**The Child's World®**
childsworld.com

Published by The Child's World®
1980 Lookout Drive • Mankato, MN 56003-1705
800-599-READ • www.childsworld.com

Photographs ©: Jonathan C. Photography/Shutterstock
Images, cover, 1, 18–19; Purestock/Thinkstock, 2–3; Shutterstock
Images, 4, 6–7; Sjoerd van der Wal/iStockphoto, 4–5;
EcoPrint/Shutterstock Images, 8–9; Mike Dexter/Shutterstock
Images, 10–11; A. Ricardo/Shutterstock Images, 12–13;
Rita Kochmarjova/Shutterstock Images, 14–15; Pavel K/
Shutterstock Images, 16; Mikhail Pogosov/Shutterstock Images,
16–17; Dennis W. Donohue/Shutterstock Images, 20–21

ISBN 9781503816787
LCCN 2016945591

Printed in the United States of America
PA02325

## ABOUT THE AUTHOR

Kurt Waldendorf is a writer and editor.
He lives in Vermont with his wife and their
Old English sheepdog, Charlie.

## NOTE FOR PARENTS AND TEACHERS

The Child's World® helps
early readers develop their
informational-reading skills by
providing easy-to-read books
that fascinate them and hold
their interest. Encourage new
readers by following these
simple ideas:

## BEFORE READING

- Page briefly through the
  book. Discuss the photos.
  What does the reader think
  he or she will learn in this
  book? Let the child ask
  questions.
- Look at the glossary
  together. Discuss the words.

## READ THE BOOK

- Now read the book
  together, or let the
  child read the book
  independently.

## AFTER READING

- Urge the child to think more.
  Ask questions such as,
  "What things are different
  among the animals shown
  in this book?"

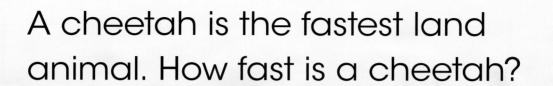

A cheetah is the fastest land animal. How fast is a cheetah?

A cheetah starts quickly. It speeds up faster than a sports car.

A cheetah reaches its top speed in just a few seconds. It runs as fast as a car on the highway.

A giraffe **gallops** with long steps. But a cheetah **dashes** almost two times faster than a giraffe.

An elephant charges with strong steps. But a cheetah can run four times faster than an elephant.

**Athletes** run fast. But even the fastest human could not beat a cheetah in a race. The cheetah would travel more than two times farther in the same amount of time.

A greyhound is the fastest dog. A cheetah reaches a greyhound's top speed in only two seconds.

A cheetah's **stride** is as long as a racehorse's. But a cheetah can take one more stride than a racehorse every second.

A cheetah does not always run in a straight line. At high speeds, a cheetah can turn faster than a motorcycle.

A cheetah uses its speed to chase its **prey**.

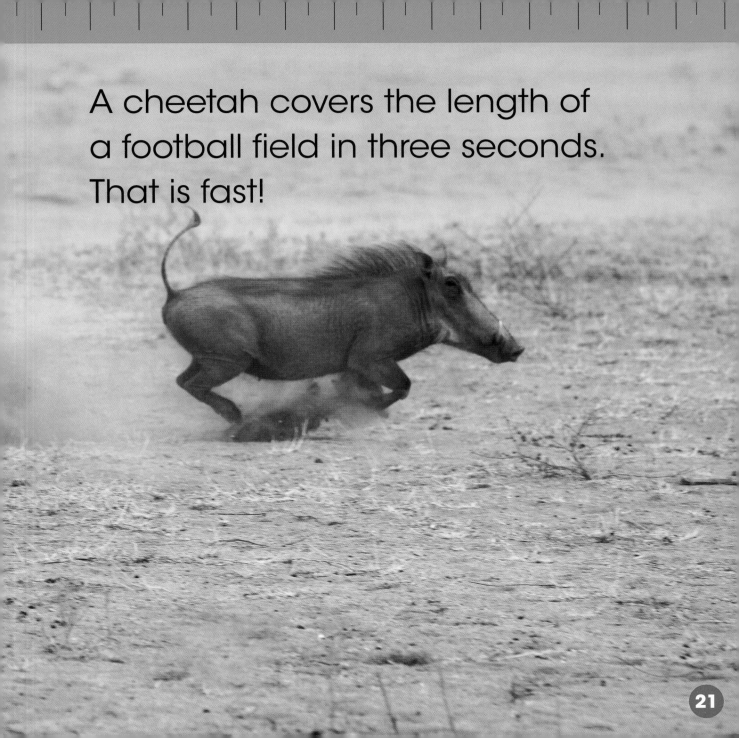

A cheetah covers the length of a football field in three seconds. That is fast!

▶ A cheetah sneaks up on its prey before chasing it.

▶ A cheetah's claws always stick out. The claws help the cheetah grip the ground.

▶ A cheetah keeps its head steady when it runs. This helps it see its prey.

▶ A cheetah has a long tail. It helps the cheetah turn at high speeds.

▶ A cheetah can run at top speed for only a few seconds. It then needs to slow down or rest.

# GLOSSARY

**athletes** (ATH-leets) Athletes are people who are good at sports. Many athletes work to become faster.

**dashes** (DASH-es) Something dashes when it moves quickly over a short distance. A cheetah dashes after other animals.

**gallops** (GAL-uhps) An animal gallops when all of its feet are off the ground as it runs. A giraffe gallops across the plain.

**prey** (PRAY) Prey is an animal that is hunted by another animal for food. A cheetah sneaks up on its prey before chasing it.

**stride** (STRIDE) A stride is an act of forward motion completed when the legs have returned to their original positions. A cheetah's stride covers a long distance.

# TO LEARN MORE

## BOOKS

Herriott, Charlotte. *Cheetah vs. Ostrich*.
New York, NY: Gareth Stevens Publishing, 2016.

Leaf, Christina. *Baby Cheetahs*.
Minneapolis, MN: Bellwether, 2015.

Ringstad, Arnold. *Cheetahs*. Mankato, MN: Amicus, 2014.

## WEB SITES

Visit our Web site for links about cheetahs:
**childsworld.com/links**

Note to Parents, Teachers, and Librarians: We routinely verify our Web links to make sure they are safe and active sites. So encourage your readers to check them out!

# INDEX